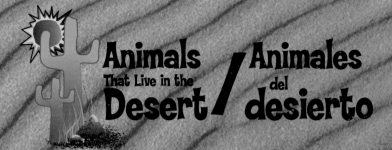

Animals That Live in the Desert / Animales del desierto

Vultures/Buitres

JoAnn Early Macken

Reading consultant/Consultora de lectura:
Susan Nations, M. Ed., author, literacy coach,
consultant/autora, tutora de alfabetización, consultora

WR WEEKLY READER
EARLY LEARNING LIBRARY

Please visit our web site at: www.earlyliteracy.cc
For a free color catalog describing Weekly Reader® Early Learning Library's list
of high-quality books, call 1-877-445-5824 (USA) or 1-800-387-3178 (Canada).
Weekly Reader® Early Learning Library's fax: (414) 336-0164.

Library of Congress Cataloging-in-Publication Data available upon request from publisher.
Fax (414) 336-0157 for the attention of the Publishing Records Department.

ISBN 0-8368-4845-4 (lib. bdg.)
ISBN 0-8368-4852-7 (softcover)

This edition first published in 2006 by
Weekly Reader® Early Learning Library
A Member of the WRC Media Family of Companies
330 West Olive Street, Suite 100
Milwaukee, WI 53212 USA

Art direction: Tammy West
Cover design and page layout: Kami Koenig
Picture research: Diane Laska-Swanke
Translators: Tatiana Acosta and Guillermo Gutiérrez

Picture credits: Cover, © Wendy Dennis/Visuals Unlimited; p. 5 © Corel;
p. 7 © Michael H. Francis; pp. 9, 15, 19 © Richard Day/Daybreak Imagery;
p. 11 © Alan & Sandy Carey; p. 13 © Lynn M. Stone; p. 17 © Elio Della Ferrera/
naturepl.com; p. 21 © Todd Fink/Daybreak Imagery

Printed in the United States of America

1 2 3 4 5 6 7 8 9 09 08 07 06 05

Note to Educators and Parents

Reading is such an exciting adventure for young children! They are beginning to integrate their oral language skills with written language. To encourage children along the path to early literacy, books must be colorful, engaging, and interesting; they should invite the young reader to explore both the print and the pictures.

Animals That Live in the Desert is a new series designed to help children read about creatures that make their homes in dry places. Each book explains where a different desert animal lives, what it eats, and how it adapts to its arid environment.

Each book is specially designed to support the young reader in the reading process. The familiar topics are appealing to young children and invite them to read — and reread — again and again. The full-color photographs and enhanced text further support the student during the reading process.

In addition to serving as wonderful picture books in schools, libraries, homes, and other places where children learn to love reading, these books are specifically intended to be read within an instructional guided reading group. This small group setting allows beginning readers to work with a fluent adult model as they make meaning from the text. After children develop fluency with the text and content, the book can be read independently. Children and adults alike will find these books supportive, engaging, and fun!

— Susan Nations, M.Ed., author, literacy coach,
and consultant in literacy development

Nota para los maestros y los padres

¡Leer es una aventura tan emocionante para los niños pequeños! A esta edad están comenzando a integrar su manejo del lenguaje oral con el lenguaje escrito. Para animar a los niños en el camino de la lectura incipiente, los libros deben ser coloridos, estimulantes e interesantes; deben invitar a los jóvenes lectores a explorar la letra impresa y las ilustraciones.

Animales del desierto es una nueva colección diseñada para que los niños lean textos sobre animales que viven en lugares muy secos. Cada libro explica dónde vive un animal del desierto, qué come y cómo se adapta a su árido medio ambiente.

Cada libro está especialmente diseñado para ayudar a los jóvenes lectores en el proceso de lectura. Los temas familiares llaman la atención de los niños y los invitan a leer —y releer— una y otra vez. Las fotografías a todo color y el tamaño de la letra ayudan aún más al estudiante en el proceso de lectura.

Además de servir como maravillosos libros ilustrados en escuelas, bibliotecas, hogares y otros lugares donde los niños aprenden a amar la lectura, estos libros han sido especialmente concebidos para ser leídos en un grupo de lectura guiada. Este contexto permite que los lectores incipientes trabajen con un adulto que domina la lectura mientras van determinando el significado del texto. Una vez que los niños dominan el texto y el contenido, el libro puede ser leído de manera independiente. ¡Estos libros les resultarán útiles, estimulantes y divertidos a niños y a adultos por igual!

— Susan Nations, M.Ed., autora/tutora de alfabetización/
consultora de desarrollo de la lectura

Vultures are large birds with long wings. They are **raptors**, birds that eat meat. Some vultures live in the desert.

- - - - - - - - - - - - - - - - -

Los buitres son aves grandes con largas alas. Son **aves rapaces**, es decir, que comen carne. Algunos buitres viven en el desierto.

Vultures do not have to kill their food. They eat dead animals. They can smell a dead animal from far away.

- - - - - - - - - - - - -

Los buitres no tienen que matar a los animales que se comen. Se alimentan de animales muertos. Los buitres pueden oler un animal muerto a

mucha distancia.

Vultures fly high in circles. They can fly for a long time. While they fly, they look for food.

Los buitres vuelan en círculo a gran altura. Pueden volar durante mucho tiempo. Mientras vuelan, los buitres buscan comida.

Vultures look for sick animals. When a sick animal dies, they eat it.

- - - - - - - - - - - - - -

Los buitres buscan animales enfermos. Cuando un animal enfermo muere, los buitres se lo comen.

Vultures have hooked bills. Their hooked bills help them tear meat apart.

- - - - - - - - - - - - - -

Los buitres tienen el pico ganchudo. La forma del pico los ayuda a desgarrar la carne.

12

bill/
pico

13

Vultures have long, thin necks.
They have few feathers on their
heads. Their heads stay clean
when they eat.

— — — — — — — — — — — —

Los buitres tienen el cuello largo
y delgado. Tienen pocas plumas
en la cabeza. Los buitres no
se ensucian la cabeza
cuando comen.

neck/
cuello

15

Vultures fight over food. They flap their wings. They poke each other with their bills. They croak and hiss.

- - - - - - - - - - - - -

Los buitres se pelean entre sí por la comida. Baten las alas y se golpean con el pico unos a otros. Mientras pelean, los buitres graznan y silban.

16

Some vultures build nests out of sticks. Some vultures do not build nests. They hide their eggs on the ground or in trees.

- - - - - - - - - - - - -

Algunos buitres usan palos para hacer nidos. Algunos buitres no hacen nidos. Esconden sus huevos en el suelo o en árboles.

18

eggs/
huevos

Baby vultures hatch from the eggs. The babies, or **chicks**, are covered with down. Their parents keep them warm. Their parents feed them meat until they can hunt on their own.

De los huevos, salen las crías de los buitres. Los bebés, o **pollos**, están cubiertos de plumón. Sus padres les dan calor. También los alimentan hasta que los pollos son capaces de cazar solos.

chicks/
pollos

GLOSSARY

bills — beaks

croak — to make a deep, hoarse sound

desert — a very dry area

down — small, soft feathers

hooked — curved

GLOSARIO

desierto — un área muy seca

ganchudo — con forma de gancho, curvado

graznar — producir un sonido grave y chillón

pico — parte delantera de la cabeza de las aves

plumón — plumas suaves y pequeñas

FOR MORE INFORMATION/ MÁS INFORMACIÓN

BOOKS IN ENGLISH

King Vultures. Animals of the Rain Forest (series). Jim Redmond (Raintree)

Vultures. Early Bird Nature Books (series). Roland Smith (Lerner Publications)

LIBROS EN ESPAÑOL

Delicious Hullabaloo/Pachanga deliciosa. Pat Mora (Piñata Books)

Pájaros. Diane James and Sara Lynn (Two-Can Publishers)

INDEX

ÍNDICE

ABOUT THE AUTHOR

JoAnn Early Macken is the author of two rhyming picture books, *Sing-Along Song* and *Cats on Judy*, and many other nonfiction books for beginning readers. Her poems have appeared in several children's magazines. A graduate of the M.F.A. in Writing for Children and Young Adults program at Vermont College, she lives in Wisconsin with her husband and their two sons. Visit her Web site at www.joannmacken.com.

INFORMACIÓN SOBRE LA AUTORA

JoAnn Early Macken ha escrito dos libros de rimas con ilustraciones, *Sing-Along Song y Cats on Judy*, y muchos otros libros de no ficción para lectores incipientes. Sus poemas han sido publicados en varias revistas infantiles. JoAnn se graduó en el programa M.F.A. de Escritura para Niños y Jóvenes de Vermont College. Vive en Wisconsin con su esposo y sus dos hijos. Puedes visitar su página web: www.joannmacken.com

24